# Papercraft Christmas Ideas

## MAGICAL CHRISTMAS CRAFTS FOR ALL AGES

# TABLE OF CONTENTS

**INTRODUCTION** — 01

**CHAPTER 1: GETTING STARTED** — 02

Essential Tools and Materials — 03
Choosing the Right Paper for Your Projects — 05
Basic Techniques — 06

**CHAPTER 2: PATTERNS** — 07

| | | | |
|---|---|---|---|
| Bulb Advent Calendar | 08 | Paper Pumpkins | 42 |
| Paper Poinsettia Lighted | 10 | Artistic Music Sheet | 45 |
| Paper Trees | 12 | Chain Advent Calendar | 48 |
| Paper Christmas Trees | 14 | Toilet Paper Roll Christmas Tree | 50 |
| Christmas Star | 16 | DIY gingerbread | 52 |
| Paper Lanterns | 19 | Toilet Roll Tube Snowflake | 54 |
| Christmas Cactus | 21 | Paper Holly Wreath | 56 |
| Mason Jar Sign | 24 | Paper Lantern | 58 |
| paper snowman | 26 | Letters to Santa Mailbox | 60 |
| Paper Honeycomb | 28 | Vintage bauble paper | 62 |
| Pine Cone | 30 | Poinsettia Ball Paper | 64 |
| Paper Star | 33 | Dove Paper | 67 |
| Flower Decor | 36 | Origami Lanterns | 69 |
| Fall Wreath | 39 | Reindeer Garland | 72 |

**CONCLUSION** — 75

# INTRODUCTION

Welcome to "Papercrafting Christmas Ideas: Magical Christmas Crafts for All Ages" This book welcomes you to the magical realm of papercrafting, where festive passion and creativity collide. There has never been a better moment to embrace the love of making and produce stunning and unforgettable creations that infuse your house with warmth and cheer than during the enchantment of Christmas.

More than just a pastime, crafting over the holidays is a great way to connect with loved ones and show your creativity. Every paper creation you make has the potential to develop into a treasured custom that is carried down through the generations. Whether you're creating tree-hanging ornaments, creating sentimental Christmas cards, or creatively wrapping presents, every little thing counts.

This book contains comprehensive directions, practical advice, and motivational ideas to help you make beautiful Christmas crafts. Every chapter covers a different facet of papercrafting, ranging from eco-friendly alternatives and gift wrapping to cards and decorations. Your creativity will be able to blossom as you master vital techniques, find new materials, and experiment with other styles.

Welcome to the wonderful world of Christmas papercrafting! Let's get started on this magical adventure!

# CHAPTER 1
# GETTING STARTED

# ESSENTIAL TOOLS AND MATERIALS

## Cutting Tools

**Craft Knife:** Perfect for intricate cuts and detailed work.

**Scissors**: A good pair of scissors is vital for general cutting tasks.

**Paper Trimmer**: Ideal for straight cuts, especially for card making and gift wrapping.

## Adhesives

**Glue Sticks:** Great for lightweight paper projects.

**Liquid Glue:** Offers strong adhesion for heavier materials.

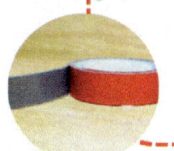

**Double-Sided Tape:** Perfect for creating a clean finish, especially for cards and decorations.

## Measuring and Marking

**Ruler**: Helps in measuring and cutting straight lines.

**Pencil**: Useful for marking measurements before cutting.

**Bone Folder:** Essential for creating crisp folds and creases.

## Decorative Tools

**Stamps and Ink:** Add beautiful designs to your projects.

**Punches**: Create shapes and designs quickly and easily.

**Embellishments**: Stickers, washi tape, and glitter can add a festive touch.

## Cutting Mats

Protect your work surface and keep your blades sharp.

# CHOOSING THE RIGHT PAPER FOR YOUR PROJECTS

 **Cardstock**: Thick and sturdy, perfect for cards, decorations, and 3D projects. It comes in various colors and textures, making it versatile for holiday crafts.

 **Patterned Paper**: Great for adding visual interest to your projects. Look for Christmas-themed patterns such as snowflakes, ornaments, and festive colors.

 **Tissue Paper**: Ideal for layering and creating delicate decorations, such as pom-poms and gift wrap.

 **Construction Paper**: A staple for children's crafts, it comes in a variety of colors and is easy to work with for simple projects.

 **Recycled Paper**: Consider using old newspapers, magazines, or scrap paper for eco-friendly crafting. This adds a unique touch to your projects and promotes sustainability.

# BASIC TECHNIQUES

### Cutting
Practice using your scissors and craft knife to achieve clean cuts. For intricate designs, start with a sharp blade and work slowly to avoid mistakes.

### Folding
Mastering the art of folding is crucial for many papercraft projects. Use a bone folder to create crisp edges, especially when making cards or paper models.

### Adhering
Familiarize yourself with different adhesives and their applications. Test them on scrap paper to understand how much glue is needed for a strong bond.

### Layering
Learn how to layer different papers for added depth and texture. Experiment with overlapping pieces and using contrasting colors to create visual interest.

### Embellishing
Add a personal touch to your projects by incorporating embellishments. Try stamping, adding stickers, or using glitter to enhance your designs.

### Experimentation
Don't be afraid to try new techniques or materials. Papercrafting is all about creativity, so let your imagination guide you.

# CHAPTER 2
## PATTERNS

# BULB ADVENT CALENDAR

## Materials

- Template
- Scissors
- Craft knife
- Glue
- Bright A4 paper and black
- Twine
- Ruler
- Numbered flags template
- Hole punch

## Instructions

- Cut out the black topper and colored bottom templates.
- Score the dotted lines with a craft knife.
- Glue the sides together using the tab.
- Cut a 6" piece of twine, string it through the top holes, and tie.
- Bend the top tabs outward and glue the black paper on top.
- Trim excess twine.
- Cut out and punch numbered flags.
- String the bulbs, placing a flag before each bulb.
- Hang your advent calendar to start counting down to Christmas!

# PAPER POINSETTIA LIGHTED

## Materials

- White Christmas lights
- Red and gold paper
- Templates (free version includes a hole in the middle)
- Full poinsettia template available for purchase
- SVG for cutting machines or outline PDF for hand cutting
- Rolling tool and molding mat
- Glue gun

## Instructions

You will need 3 large petal cuts and 2 small as shown.

Use your rolling tool to create veins on all the petals.

Use your rolling tool to create veins on all the petals.

Layer the first 3 pieces on top each other alternating petals.

Add to the two smaller petal cuts.

If you are not doing the lighted garland then you can add some pearls as center accents.

# PAPER TREES

### Materials

- Black & White Paper
- Black Crystal Beads
- Clear Crystal Beads
- Glue Stick
- Jewelry Making Wire

# Instructions

1. Cut out the trees and fold in half. Fold your decorative paper in half and trace the half tree, lining up on the fold. Cut out.

2. I cut out eight tree shapes.

3. Add glue to half of the tree and attach second piece to the first. Keep moving around the tree.

4. Add a strip of wire along the seam with extra wire extending out the top of the tree before attaching the final piece. String beads onto top of wire.

5.

# PAPER CHRISTMAS TREES

### Materials

- Adjustable circle cutter
- Green card stock (Mohawk Felt Leaf Green #C12355 and Esse Texture Verde #C1650, 8 1/2"-by-11")
- Bone folder
- Scissors
- Wooden skewers
- Wooden spools
- Gold beads
- Hot-glue gun and glue sticks
- Craft knife (Martha Stewart Craft Knife)

## Instructions

1. For large Christmas trees, use an adjustable circle cutter to make 2-, 3-, 4-, 5-, and 6-inch-diameter circles from green card stock (for small trees, omit the 6-inch circle).

2. Fold each circle in half four times with a bone folder. While circles are folded, snip off the tip of each piece using a craft knife, forming a very small hole in the center.

3. Place smallest circle on the pointed end of a wooden skewer (we used 12-inch skewers), letting the tip poke through the hole in circle. With a hot-glue gun, dab underside of circle, where paper and skewer meet. Hold for 10 seconds to secure.

4. Working one at a time from smallest circle to largest, slide remaining circles onto the skewer; secure with glue.

5. Insert the bottom of skewer into a spool; remove, and cut skewer to desired height (we cut ours to 6, 9, and 10 inches), keeping in mind that only spool should be visible beneath the standing tree. Return skewer to spool; secure with glue. Add a dot of glue to top of skewer, and attach a gold bead.

# CHRISTMAS STAR

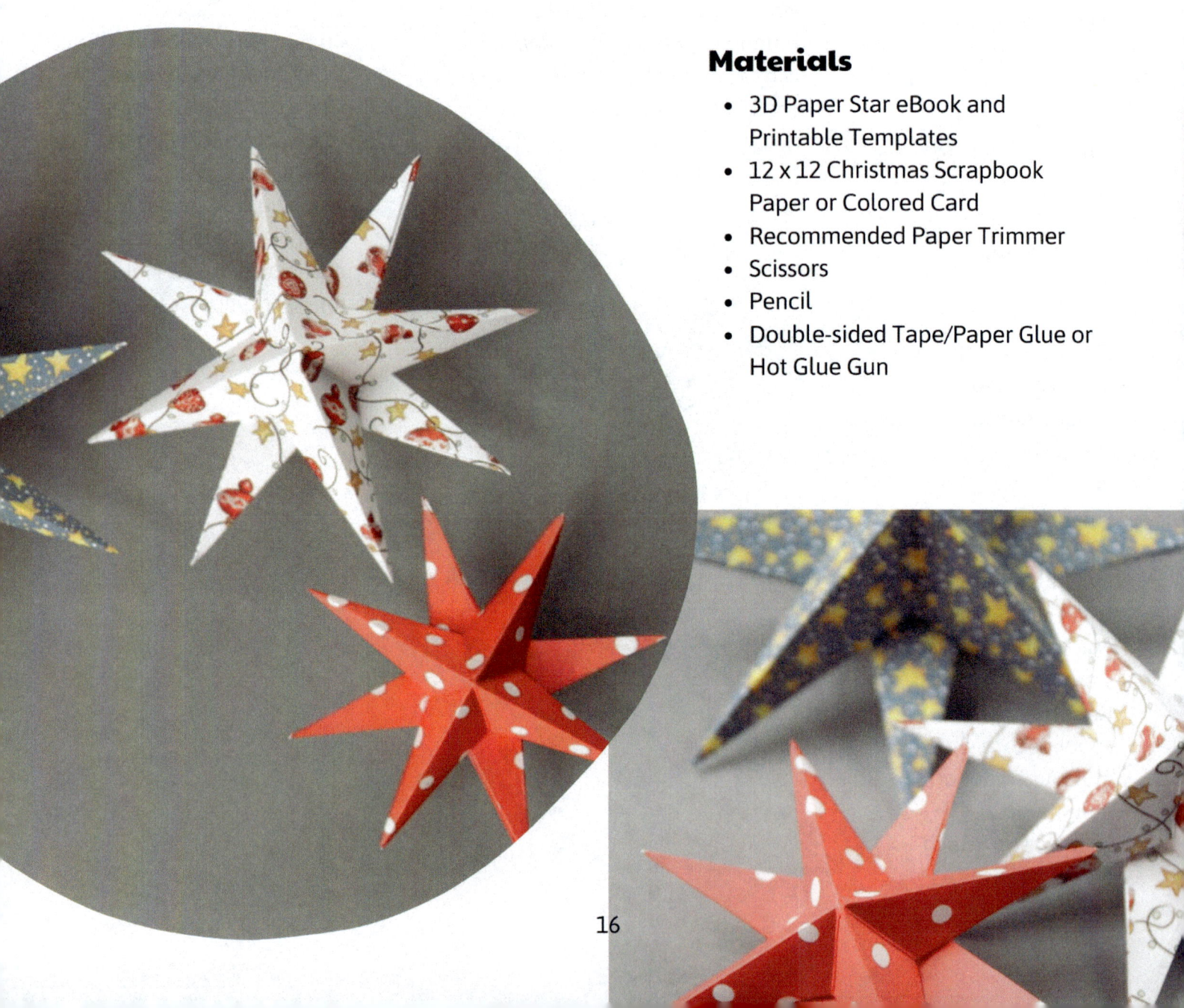

## Materials

- 3D Paper Star eBook and Printable Templates
- 12 x 12 Christmas Scrapbook Paper or Colored Card
- Recommended Paper Trimmer
- Scissors
- Pencil
- Double-sided Tape/Paper Glue or Hot Glue Gun

## Instructions

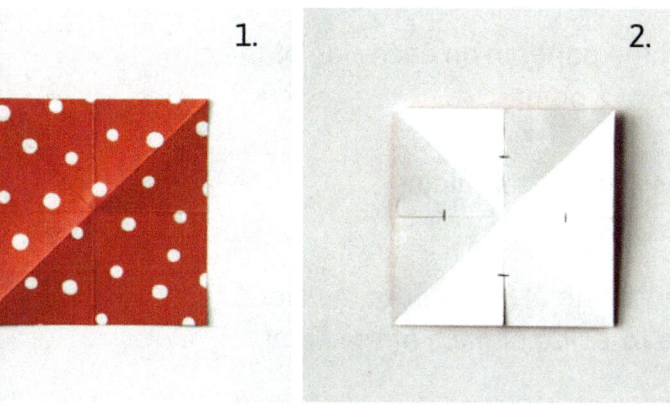

1.
2.

- Take a square of paper and fold it in half. For the large star, I used a piece of 12x12 inch scrapbook paper. To make a different size star cut your paper or card stock to a smaller or larger size.

- Open out, rotate 90 degrees and fold in half again.

- Open out and fold your paper in half again this time along both diagonals.

3.
4.

- Flip the paper over and mark a little less than halfway down each of the horizontal and vertical creases.

- Cut down to the pencil marks.
- If you are not doing the lighted garland then you can add some pearls as center accents.

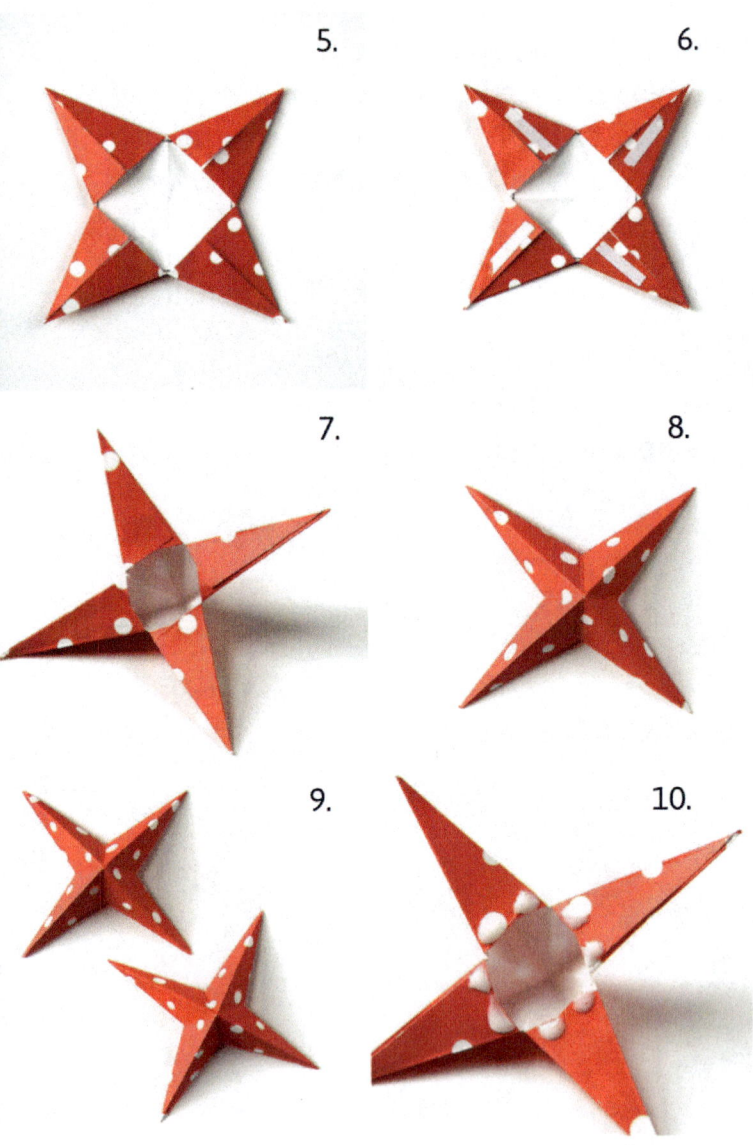

- Fold the paper in on each side of the cut to form a point.

- Repeat on all remaining sides.

- Apply a line of glue or double-sided tape to 1 side of each of the points.

- Peel back the tape and fold 1 side of the point over the other and stick down.

- Do the same on the remaining points to make a four-pointed star shape. This will make half your star.

- Repeat the steps above to make the 2nd half.

- Apply some more glue to the centre corners of each point.

# PAPER LANTERNS

### Materials

- Paper lantern cut files
- Cover stock
- Spray paint
- Plexiglass sheets
- X-acto knife
- Battery powered candles
- Hot glue gun and glue sticks
- Electronic cutting machine (Silhouette Cameo or Cricut)

## Instructions

 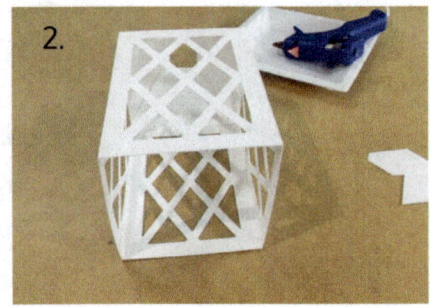 

- Cut out the pieces you need for your lantern.
- Fold the side pieces so they form a box.
- Glue the two pieces together at the tabs. Fold the top of the side pieces so they form a pyramid on the top.
- Glue the tabs to secure.
- Fold the square base and glue it together at the tab.
- Place a bead of glue on the bottom of the top box and secure it to the top of the pyramid.
- Shape the very top piece.
- Spray paint the lantern with the color of your choice.
- Use plexiglass or clear plastic craft sheets on the inside of the DIY paper lanterns and attach with hot glue.

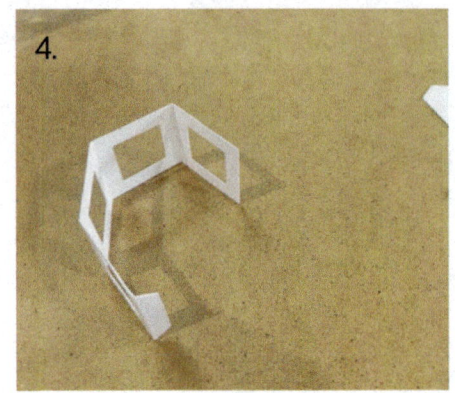

# CHRISTMAS CACTUS

### Materials

- Green text weight paper
- Red tissue paper
- Scrap paper
- Pot of your choice
- Gravel or sand
- Wire cutters
- Green paper covered wire
- Scissors
- Bone folder
- Elmer's x-treme glue stick
- Foam
- Knife
- Green corsage tape
- Masking tape

## Instructions

Make the flowers for your cactus! You can make one for each stem, or apply them more sparingly and just add a few to your plant. First, cut a piece of tissue paper approximately 2.5" x 10". Next, fold it in half and in half again, keep folding until your tissue paper is about ½" wide. Cut one end to a point.

Apply a line of glue stick along the straight edge of the tissue and begin to wrap around one end of your wire. You'll be pinching and lightly folding as you go to achieve a more dimensional flower shape. Finish it off by applying a length of corsage tape.

Cut your cactus stems (either with your craft cutter or by tracing and cutting by hand). You'll need 2 matching paper cut outs for each stem. Apply a heavy layer of glue stick and place the wire directly in the center. Apply a layer of glue to the other piece and carefully sandwich the wire in between, making sure the sides line up.

4.

Next, use your bone folder (old credit card also works) to burnish around the edges of the wire. You'll want to do this while the glue is still wet. Press around the wire on both sides, making sure it's secure. Set aside to dry.

While your stems are drying, you can prep your pot! Cut a piece of foam to fit inside (about 1" from the top) and use the masking tape to hold it in place. Cover the foam with gravel or sand.

5.

6.

Start assembling your plant! You can bend the wire to give it some personality!

# MASON JAR SIGN

## Materials

- Unfinished Wooden Sign
- White Chalk Paint
- Black Adhesive Craft Vinyl
- Silhoutte Cuting Machine
- Transfer Tape
- Hot Glue Gun, Gluesticks
- Mason Jar Cut File
- Pointsettia Cut File
- Pine Branches Cut File
- Red Glitter Cardstock
- Red Cardstock
- Green Cardstock
- Beads or Gems
- Buffalo Check Ribbon

## Instructions

Paint the wood sign and let dry completely. Cut the mason jar shape out of black craft vinyl. Weed excess vinyl.

Apply mason jar design to wood using transfer tape.

Cut out flowers. Layer the flowers and glue them. Add small decorations to the centers. Cut out green holly leaves and pine branches.

Arrange the flowers and greenery so they look like they're coming out of the top of the mason jar. Glue into place using hot glue. Add a bow if desired.

Choose a festive holiday word and cut it out of adhesive vinyl. Weed excess vinyl.

Apply the word to the wood sign using transfer tape.

# PAPER SNOWMAN

**Materials**

- Good quality A4 paper
- Scissors
- Ruler
- Something pointy (to score your paper with)
- Glue

## Instructions

Make sure you set your printing preferences to 'photo' and 'best photo'. Cut around the outside of the body, head and nose.

Take the head and score along the light grey lines using a ruler and pointy object (such as compass or needle). Fold along each of these lines. Glue together.

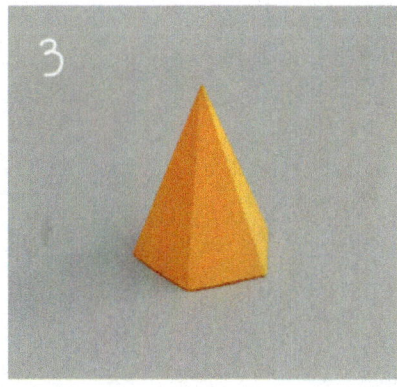

Cut and fold the nose.

Glue the nose onto the head and the head onto the body.

# PAPER HONEYCOMB

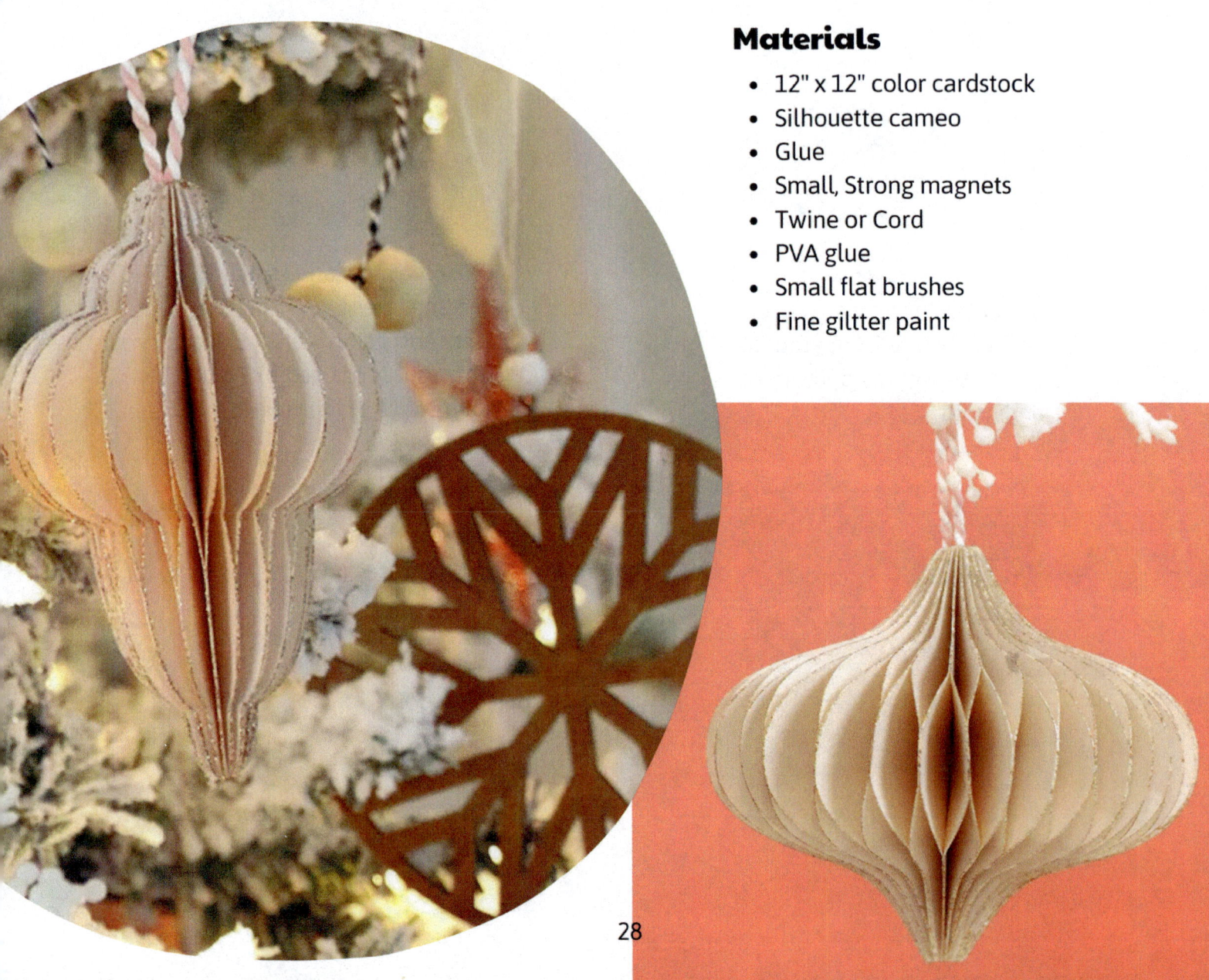

**Materials**

- 12" x 12" color cardstock
- Silhouette cameo
- Glue
- Small, Strong magnets
- Twine or Cord
- PVA glue
- Small flat brushes
- Fine giltter paint

## Instructions

Cut Ornament Pieces.

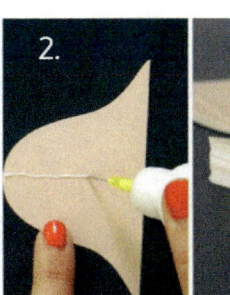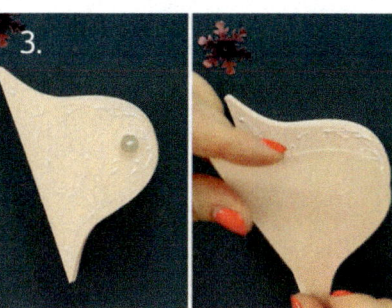

Stack and Glue Pieces Together.

Add Magnets.

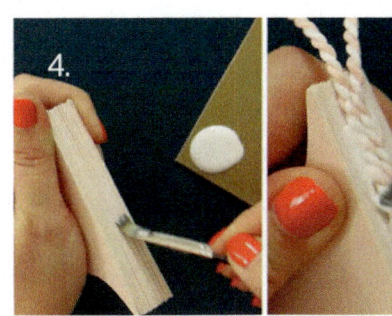

Add Twine and Seal Inner Edge.

Add some sparkle!

Well done!

# PINE CONE

**Materials**

- 12 X 12 scrapbook paper (one per ornament)
- Paper cutter
- Tape
- Hot glue and glue gun
- Twine
- Ribbon
- Scissors

## Instructions

  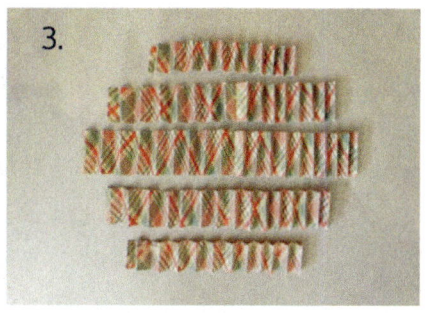

To maximize the use of paper, first cut 12" strips as follows:
- 2- 1" strips
- 4- 1.25" strips
- 2- 1.5" strips

Next, make the following cuts (see photo below):
- The 2- 1" strips will stay the same at 1"X 12"
- Next, the 2- 1.25" strips will each be cut into 2 – 8" strips
- The 2- 1.5" strips will each be cut into 2 – 10" strips

Tape the corresponding strips together as shown below.

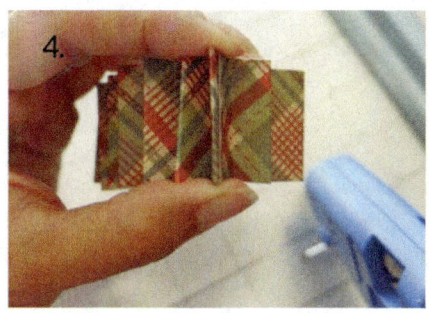 

Fold each strip like an accordion.

Use hot glue to glue the ends of each strip together. Here is a top and side view.

Next, bend the circle strip inward to form a medallion. Add a drop of hot glue in the middle and hold the medallion together for a few seconds until the glue is dry. Blowing helps!

After that, hot glue each layer together to form a sphere as shown.

Next, cut a piece of twine or ribbon and hot glue it to the top of the ornament for the hanger. Hot glue works the best because it dries quickly.

Lastly, Tie a ribbon bow around the top.

# PAPER STAR

### Materials
- Scissors
- Hot glue
- A pencil
- Silver paper
- A ruler

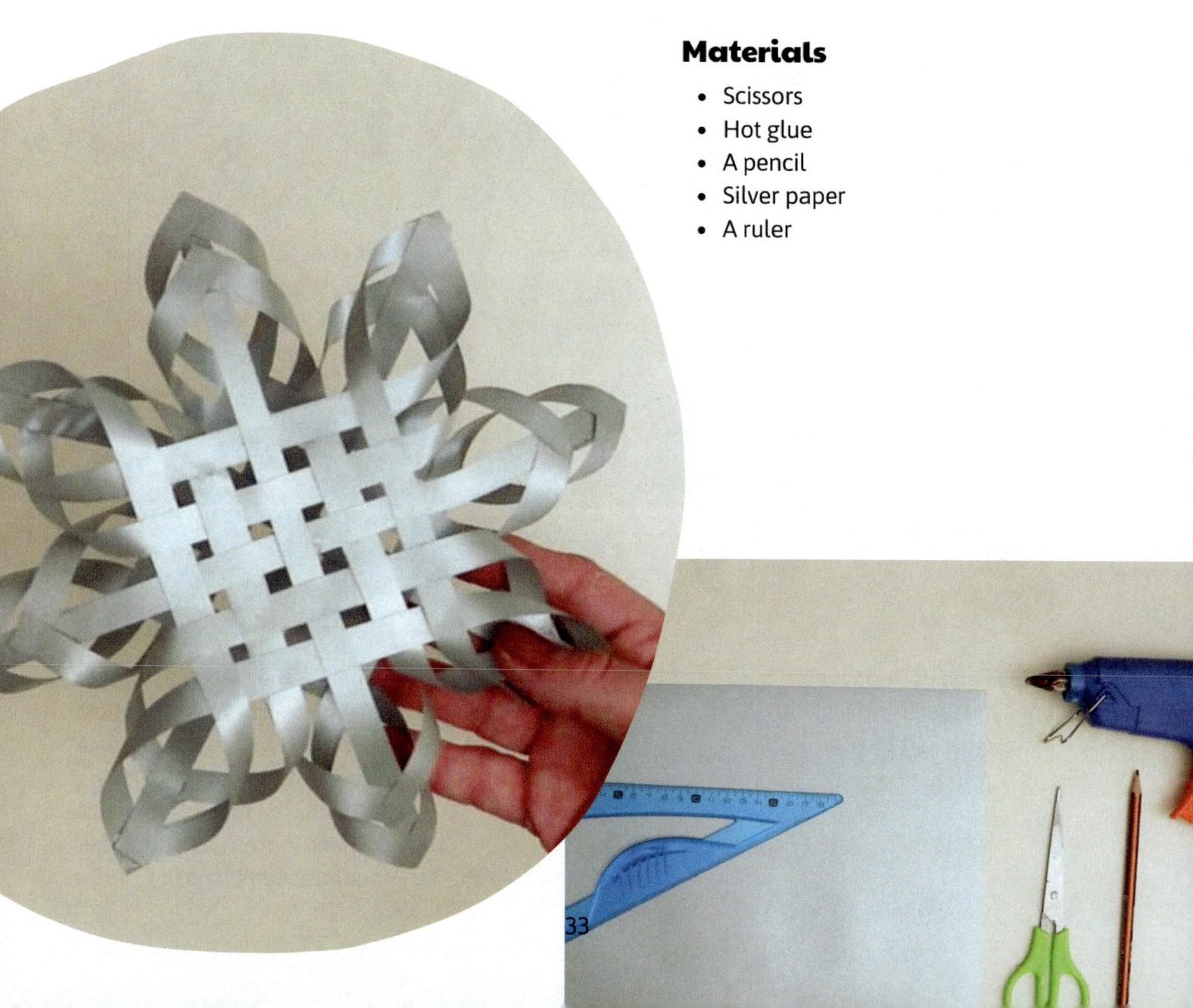

## Instructions

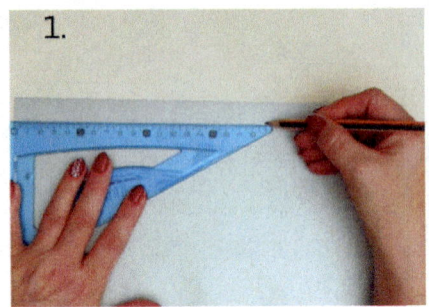

1. Draw your lines.

2. Draw vertical lines.

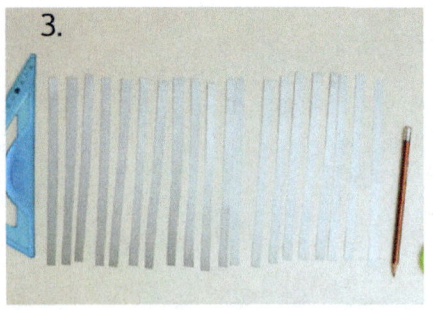

3. Cut out each strip from your page, keeping your scissors straight along each of your drawn lines.

4. Adjust and position them until you feel like things sit evenly in a sort of grid.

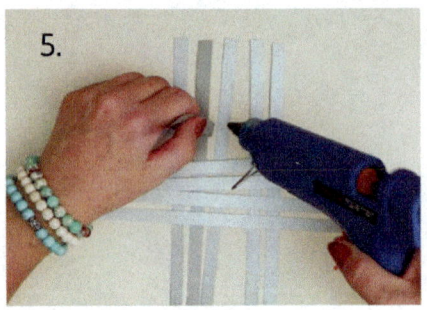

5. Glue.

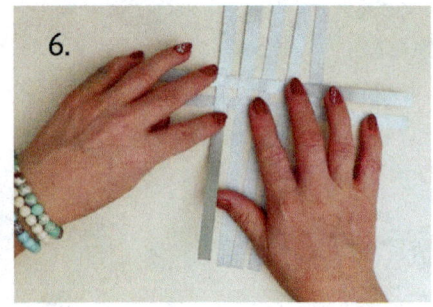

6. Repeat the above basket weaving process almost exactly, with the same alternating and gluing technique that we just outlined, only using your other four horizontal strips.

7. Repeat the entire overlapping, weaving, and gluing process with your second set of ten strips that you set aside earlier, split into groups of five and laid vertically and horizontally in the same way as before.

8. Start joining the ends.

9. Repeat the loop process once more all the way around

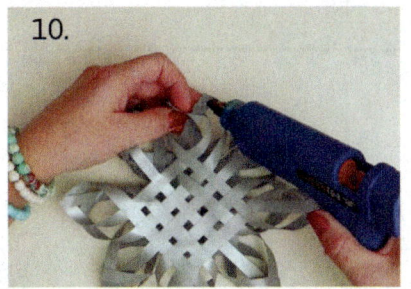

10. It's time to join your loops

# FLOWER DECOR

### Materials

- 2 sheets of patterned scrapbooking paper
- Paper trimmer
- Hot glue gun
- 2-inch paper punch
- Embellishment for the ornament center
- Ribbon

## Instructions

1.

To begin, trim (14) 1-inch squares from one of your sheets of patterned paper using your paper trimmer. From the other sheet, trim (14) 1.25-inch squares.

To form each of the petals for your flower, you will first fold over one corner, as shown...

2.

3.

...and then fold over the opposite corner, so the two sides overlap at the center and your square is now a cone shape. At the point where the two sides overlap, secure them together with a small dab of hot glue. Repeat this process until all of your squares are folded.

Now, cut a 2-inch circle from one of your sheets of patterned paper, and mark the center with a pen.

4.

Working in small sections, apply a line of hot glue to the outer edge of your circle piece, and start adhering your larger petal pieces to the circle base, making sure the points of each petal are precisely aligned with the mark you drew in the previous step.

Keep working until all of your larger petals are adhered to the circle base. When you get to the end of this process, you might not have room for the 14th petal, depending on how close your other petals are together. That is absolutely fine.

Adhere your smaller petals in the same manner, directly on top of the bottom petal layer. Adhere these smaller petals so that they are staggered in between the larger ones below.

# FALL WREATH

## Materials

- 9" wooden embroidery hoop
- Silhouette cutting machine
- Rose gold craft vinyl
- "Hello Fall" Silhouette cut file
- Transfer tape
- Metallic/glitter scrapbook papers (gold, copper, champagne, bronze, rose gold)
- Ribbon (from Hobby Lobby)
- Hot glue gun + glue sticks

## Instructions

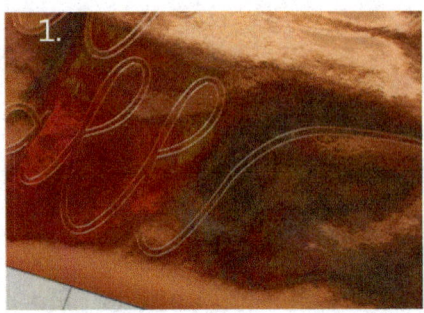  

**Step 1:** We'll start by making the words that go inside the wreath. You can download the words I created (link in supply list above) or use the "Offset" tool in Silhouette Studio to create your own words with an outline layer. Cut the back shadow layer out of cardstock, then cut the top layer from rose gold vinyl.

**Step 2:** Once the two layers are combined, place them inside the embroidery hoop. Attach the words with hot glue at the four edges where the swooshes touch the hoop.

**Step 3:** Adjust the cut settings and send them to the machine. Note that glitter cardstock is quite thick and will need a pretty deep blade setting to get a clean cut.

## Instructions

**Step 4:** After all of your leaves are cut, it's time to shape them to look more realistic. If you have an embossing tool, that would work well. If not, the rounded end of a paint brush handle works well. That's what I used. Place the leaves on a soft work surface like a self-healing mat or a folded up dish towel, then use the tip to press veins into each leaf.

**Step 5:** Use hot glue to attach the leaves to the embroidery hoop.

**Step 6:** Add a ribbon to the top of the wreath for hanging, then find the perfect spot to hang your pretty new fall decoration!

# PAPER PUMPKINS

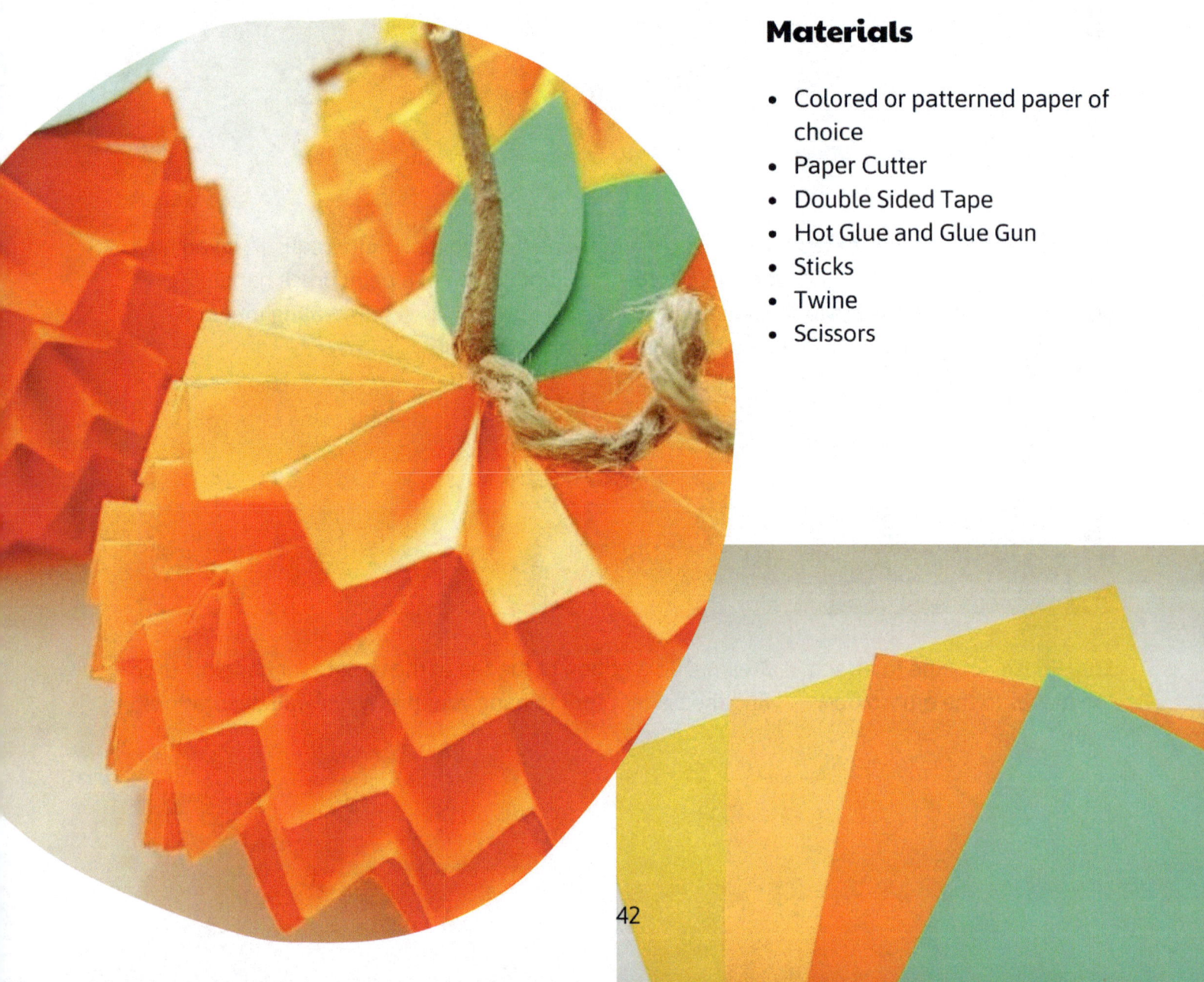

**Materials**

- Colored or patterned paper of choice
- Paper Cutter
- Double Sided Tape
- Hot Glue and Glue Gun
- Sticks
- Twine
- Scissors

## Instructions

Cut each piece of paper vertically into five 1.5" wide strips.

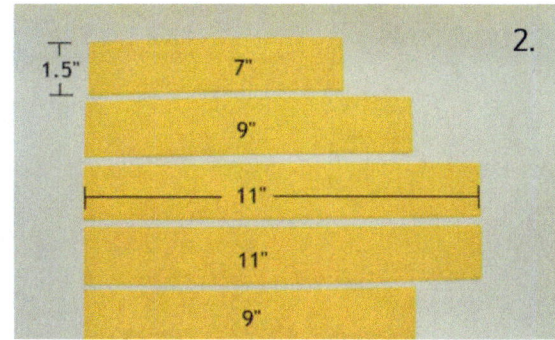

Then cut each strip into one 7", two 9", and keep the remaining two at 11". Important: Remember, you need two sets for one pumpkin. So each pumpkin is two pieces of paper – two 7", four 9", and four 11" strips.

Fold each piece into accordion strips. Pictured here is one sheet of paper.

Next tape the TWO SETS at same lengths together with double sided tape and form a circle.

You will end up with one circle from the 7" strips, two circles from the 9" strips, and two circles from the 11" strips.

Create the 7" medallion by gluing with a hot glue gun. Just place a small dab in the center and hold a few seconds until it is dry.

Next, glue each medallion together respectively starting with the 7" on top, then 9", then 11", then 11", then 9" on the bottom.

Hot glue a stick, paper leaves, and twine on the top of your pumpkin.

# ARTISTIC MUSIC SHEET

## Materials

- Old sheet music
- Dowel rod
- Wooden slice for base
- Mini gold star stickers
- Tools
- Scissors
- Hot glue gun and glue

## Instructions

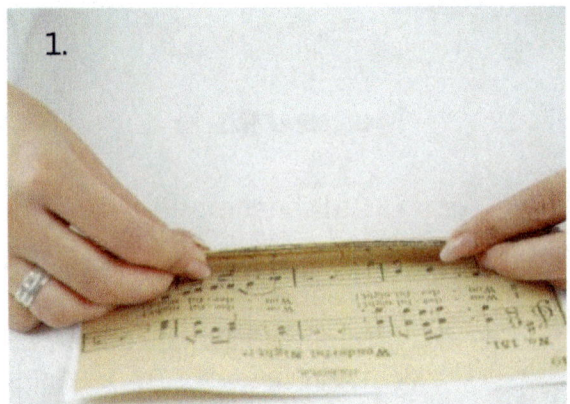

Begin by folding your sheet music into a paper fan shape. I do this on the shorter side of the paper so your tree is nice and tall.

Once you have folded the paper, you will trim it into a tree shape; You can do this easily by unfolding and then folding the paper into a triangle and cutting along the creases.

Next, you will need to cut small holes every few folds of the paper so you can insert your dowel rod through the center.

I did this by using a small knife and making a simple "x" so it could simply push through and fit the rod perfectly;

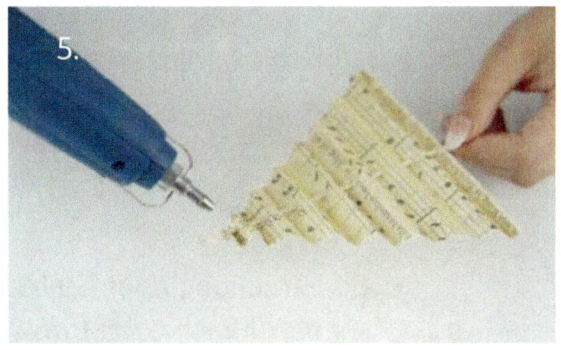

Once you have the holes, you will slide the dowel rod through the paper gently and pull up to create the tree shape;You can then trim off any excess wood, and use a bit of hot glue to secure on the top and bottom;

Next, glue or secure a small gold star to the top of your tree;

The final step before displaying is to hot glue the dowel rod onto the center of your wood slice (or whatever you choose to use as a base).

Display your tree on a mantle, as a centerpiece, or on a bookshelf

# CHAIN ADVENT CALENDAR

## Materials

- Construction paper - at least four sheets of each color (brown and white)
- Craft foam - black, orange, and brown
- Craft glue
- Adhesive wiggle eyes
- Ribbon, small wreath, pom poms, or other embellishments
- Scissors
- Pen or pencil
- Ruler
- Stapler

**Instructions**

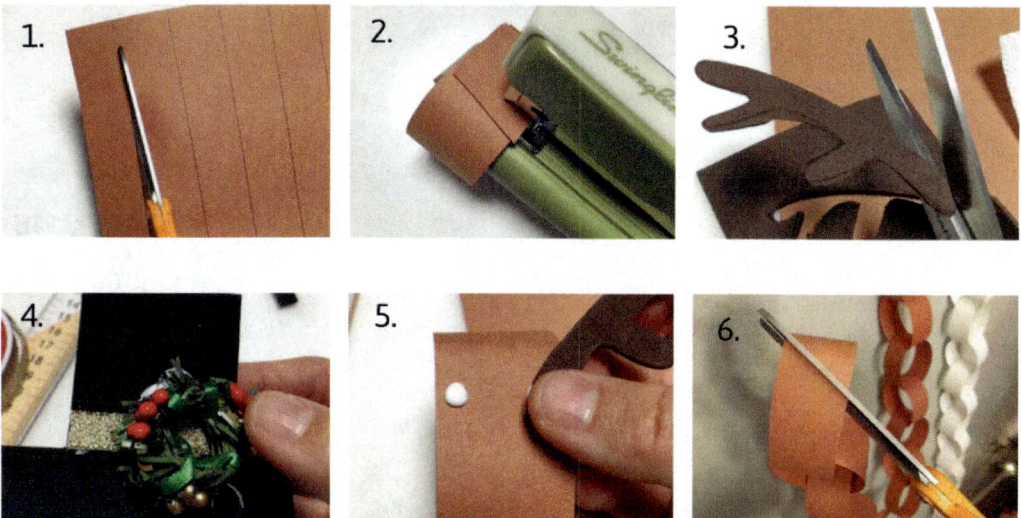

1. On the construction paper, place the ruler parallel to the short side and trace down the right side of the ruler.
2. Move the ruler over and place the left side on the pen line, then draw another line down the right side of the ruler.
3. Keep going until the whole paper is sectioned off. You'll get about 8 - 9 strips per sheet of construction paper.
4. Cut out all the strips. You're going to want 26 strips total - 25 rings for the countdown and then one for the head.
5. Use a stapler to turn 24 of the paper strips into rings, attaching them in a row. Staple the 25th ring but don't attach it, and leave the 26th paper strip alone.
6. Draw out your embellishments (like antlers or a hat) directly onto the craft foam. Then cut out using the scissors.
7. Add fun embellishments if you want to, like ribbon and a mini wreath.
8. To the lone rings, add your embellishments with craft glue (the hat, the antlers, the noses, etc.). Let them dry. Then attach them to the main ring chain with the last paper strip.
9. Hang your chains on the wall near your tree or in a place where the kids can reach.
10. You'll have them use their scissors to cut off one of the rings every single day from December 1st through Christmas morning.

# TOILET PAPER ROLL CHRISTMAS TREE

**Materials**

- Empty toilet paper rolls and paper towel rolls
- Marker or pencil for sketching tree shapes
- Craft paint of choice
- Scissors

## Instructions

1. Take your cardboard rolls and flatten them a little so you know where to draw your tree.
2. Draw your tree shape on the cardboard however you want it to look. Make sure to leave a bottom for your tree to stand up with. I left the bottoms of my rolls about 1-2 cms in height.
3. Start cutting around your lines, but be sure to have the roll still connected on some parts of the tree. This will help with the balance of the tree and for painting when the cardboard gets wet.
4. Once your shape is cut out, "fluff" out your tree a little so the bottom part is rounded again and is able to stand up. I had to pinch/fold it the opposite way it was folded before to bring it back to shape.
5. Grab your favorite paint colors you want to paint your trees and get creative!
6. When you're done set them up on your mantle, or in little vignettes around your house. I put them next to some ceramic white houses we pull out each year and I love how they contrast next to the houses. You can also use battery operated candles to put inside them to light them up. I used some copper while lights we had and intertwined them in the trees and houses and I love the simple, magical look to it all!

# DIY GINGERBREAD

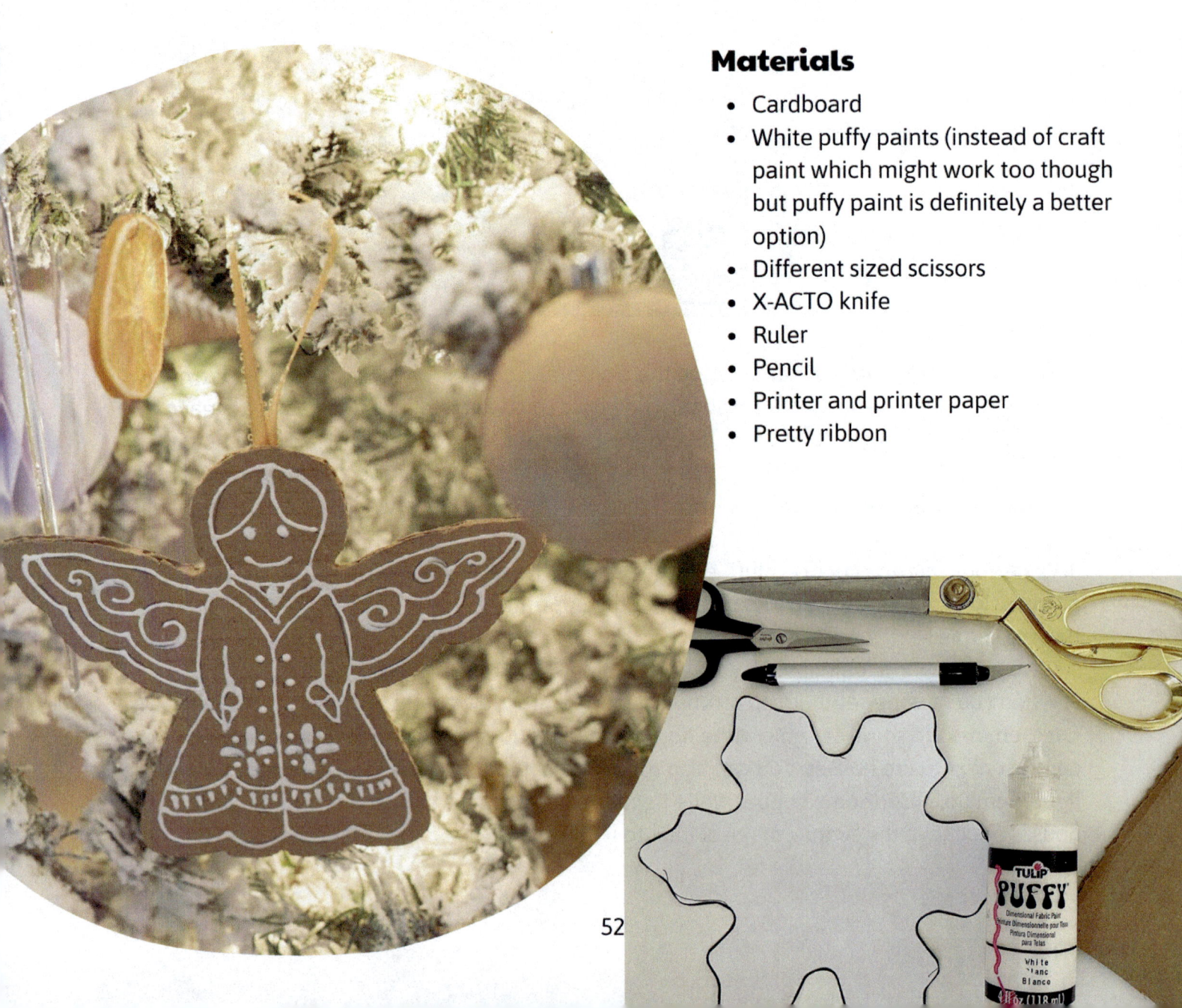

**Materials**

- Cardboard
- White puffy paints (instead of craft paint which might work too though but puffy paint is definitely a better option)
- Different sized scissors
- X-ACTO knife
- Ruler
- Pencil
- Printer and printer paper
- Pretty ribbon

## Instructions

1. Prepare your gingerbread templates

2. Trace your template onto cardboard with a pencil

3. Cut out Gingerbread shapes

4. Draw on gingerbread design pattern

5. Trace the gingerbread pattern with puffy paint

6. Add ribbon for hanging

# TOILET ROLL TUBE SNOWFLAKE

**Materials**

- 3 toilet rolls
- Ruler
- Pencil
- Scissors
- Glue gun
- String

## Instructions

1. Flatten one of the toilet rolls so that there is a fold on each side
2. Use the ruler and pencil to draw horizontal lines 1 centimetre apart.
3. Follow the lines to cut 1-centimetre strips (creating a series of loops)
3. Arrange the loops into a flower shape to form the centre of the flower and glue the tips together
4. Flatten another toilet roll and repeat step 2. And then cut the strips in half horizontally and use the glue to create smaller loops. Attach these to the flower using glue
5. Flatten a third toilet roll and repeat step 2. Cut the loop open to create an arch and then attach these to the flower with glue.
6. Add string to hang your decoration

# PAPER HOLLY WREATH

### Materials

- Holly leaves cut files
- Light Green Cardstock
- 5" embroidery hoop
- Green floral wire
- Green floral tape
- Optional: Silhouette Cameo
- Hot glue gun and glue sticks

## Instructions

1. Print the holly leaves onto a light green cardstock.
2. Fold the leaves along the dotted lines.
3. Curl the edge of the leaves by rolling the points around the side of a pencil.
4. Glue a 3" piece of floral wire to the back of each leaf.
5. Run a bead of hot glue along the center ridge, then press the floral wire into it.
6. Bend the bottom of the floral wire and give it a slight curve.
7. Add glue to the side of the floral wire and press the folded over piece into it.
8. Continue all around the wreath until you have added all the holly leaves.
9. Wrap the embroidery hoop with floral tape.
10. Shape the wreath by folding down the wire to make the leaves sweep around the hoop.
11. Fold and tweak until you like the shape.
12. Leave as is, or add red wire to give a pop of color to the wreath.

# PAPER LANTERN

**Materials**

- Paper lantern cut files
- Cardstock
- Twine
- Battery powered tea lights
- Hot glue gun and glue sticks
- Silhouette Cameo

## Instructions

Cut out the paper lantern ornament template from the cardstock.

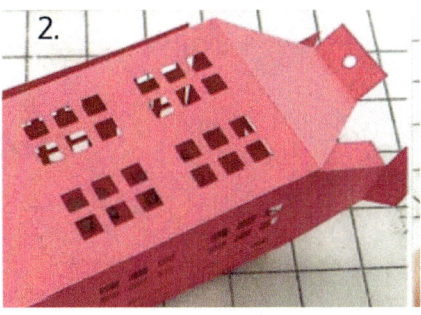

Fold along all the dotted lines.

Glue the flap on the side to create a square shape.

Glue the flaps on the bottom to one side, followed by the second bottom side flap. Glue the flap on the side to create a square shape.

Then glue the flaps on the bottom to one side, followed by the second bottom side flap.

Secure the flaps around the top angled part first, then finish with the very top of the paper lantern. Thread a piece of twine into the holes at the top and tie for hanging.

# LETTERS TO SANTA MAILBOX

**Materials**

- Santa mailbox template
- Glitter cardstock
- Hot glue gun and glue sticks
- Twine or ribbon
- Optional: Electronic cutting machine

# Instructions

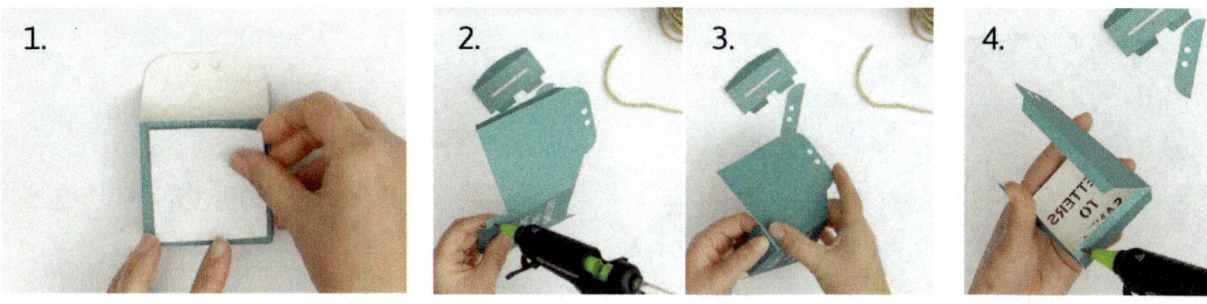

1. Cut out the pieces for 2 mailboxes on each 8 1/2" x 11" sheet of paper.
2. Once cut, fold along all the dotted lines to prepare for glue.
3. Measure inside the fold lines on the front of the mailbox and cut a piece of paper just smaller than it.
4. Add glue to one of the flaps starting at the bottom of the mailbox.
5. Secure it to the bottom side.
6. Finish by gluing the tabs to close up the entire mailbox piece.
7. Attach the top of the mailbox by sliding the tabs into the slots on the back.
8. Face the flaps toward the top of the mailbox to keep the top angled properly.
9. Glue to the back of the ornament to secure.
10. Add glue to the top piece over the front of the back to cover up any exposed back.
11. Cut a piece of twine or ribbon to make a loop through the two holes on the top.
12. Tie it to secure.

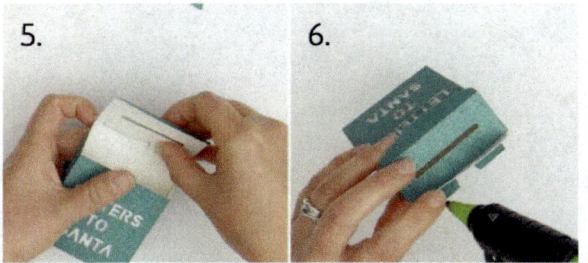

# VINTAGE BAUBLE PAPER

## Materials

- Paper Christmas decoration templates
- Gold, cream, pale blue, purple pearlescent paper
- Green card
- Paper straw
- Adhesives
- Mini polystrene balls, beads or gems, sequins
- Gold thread & needle

## Instructions

1. Use the paper Christmas decoration templates to cut the following for each bauble:
   - 9 x paper strips – gold pearlescent paper
   - 9 x paper strips – contrasting pearlescent paper
   - 2 x caps – gold pearlescent paper
   - 1 x leaf – green card
2. Thread a needle with gold thread and double up, knotting to leave a few strands of gold thread to hang, pierce needle through centre of 1 of the cap pieces and gently push all the way through to thread it onto the end of the thread to sit on the knot.
3. Thread the needle through the lower end of each paper strip in turn, (about half a centimetre from the end), alternating the colours as you go until all 18 strips are threaded.
4. Cut a piece of paper straw approx 1.5" and thread the needle through it, it will sit on the threaded strips and become a spacer / support piece later.
5. Now thread the other end of each paper strip back through the needle in turn, starting with the first strip and working your way through as before, they will spread out as you work to create a bauble shape.
6. When you have finished threading all the strips, pull the thread so the bauble shape is supported by the paper straw inside and thread the needle through a sequin, tying to secure, don't cut thread.
7. To finish, glue a green holly or mistletoe leaf to the other gold cap piece and add 3 berries, pierce a hole in the cap with the needle and thread it onto the gold thread, followed by another gold sequin, secure in place with a gentle knot. Remove needle, tie ends of gold thread to create hanging loop.

# POINSETTIA BALL PAPER

## Materials
- Red, green and yellow card
- Ribbon
- Sequins

## Instructions

Use the paper Christmas decoration templates to cut the following

Adhere 1 red flower on top of another, offsetting to create a layered flower

Repeat to create 12 layered flowers.

Take the green connecting flowers and bend up the outer looped edges towards you, and the solid petals downwards slightly, do this for all 12 green connecting flowers.

Take 1 layered red flower and place on top of a green connecting flower, glue 1 petal point of the lower red flower onto the centre of the green loop petal only.

Do this for all 5 red petals on the bottom layer of the flower, so each is attached to it's green looped petal below.

7.

Take 6 of the flowers and turn upside down, place one in the centre and arrange the 5 other flowers around it so the solid green petals line up with a corresponding solid petal.

8.

Add glue to the end part of a green petal on the centre piece and glue a corresponding petal from another flower to it, lining up the petals, nipping together and bending to ensure they are secured. Continue to attach each flower to the centre flower.

9.

Now attach each of the flowers to it's neighbouring flower using the side petals, continue until all 5 flowers are attached and the shape now resembles a half ball.

10.

Repeat steps 8 to 10 with the remaining 6 flower pieces to create 2 half ball shapes.

11.

Join the 2 half together in the same way as previously, simply glueing each petal to it's corresponding petal on the other half.

12.

To finish, adhere a circle of yellow card and 3 small polystyrene balls, sequins or beads to each flower centre and thread with a cord or ribbon for hanging.

# DOVE PAPER

## Materials

- Paper Christmas decorations templates
- White, Green, & Gold Card
- Adhesives
- Adhesive Gems and Glitter Glue to decorate
- Gold Cord or Ribbon to hang

## Instructions

1. Using the paper Christmas decorations templates, cut the following shapes for each dove
2 x main body – white card
2 x inner body layer – white card
2 x large heart – white card
2 x small heart – gold card
6 x leaf shapes – green card
We've included suggestions for the colour of materials for each shape, but swap in other paper scraps and colours to make this project if you prefer!

2. Using glitter glue, edge the 2 inner body layers to add sparkle to the outline, and leave to dry.

3. When dry, adhere the inner body layers centrally onto the main body pieces, leave the tips of the tail and wing feathers unglued to allow them to be bent slightly with your fingers to give more dimension.

4. Cover the beak section with a small piece of gold card and trim flush with body piece.

5. For a folded wing, score along the wing line using a scoring board or gently crease with your fingers.

6. Glue 2 leaf stalks to each of the body pieces. Layer up the gold heart and white heart and adhered in the centre of the leaf stalks, raising slightly with a foam pad if desired.

7. Layer up 2 leaf pieces back to back to strengthen and glue in place behind the beak on 1 of the body pieces, create a loop of gold cord and adhere on the back of 1 of the body pieces, centrally behind the wing.

8. Adhere the other side of the body in place, lining up carefully and pressing firmly all around to secure.

9. To finish, add dark blue adhesive gems for eyes and crystal gems to decorate the tail pieces.

# ORIGAMI LANTERNS

## Materials

- Two sheets of A4 paper (we used Kitty McCall Encinitas Gift Wrap cut to size, available from www.kittymccall.com)
- Ribbon, 30cm (11⅞")
- Washi tape (read our guide to washi tape if you want to learn more)
- Hole punch
- LED tealights

## Instructions

1. Take one sheet of A4 paper and fold it into 16 equal sections across the length. Unfold, then fold each crease in the opposite direction, creating concertina folds across the length of the sheet.

2. Using a ruler, draw two horizontal lines on the back of the paper, one 9cm (3⅝") down from the top long edge, and one 12cm (4¾") down.

3. Crease zig-zagged diagonals between each horizontal fold, inside the marked pencil lines. It can help to press the paper against the edge of a ruler to get a more accurate fold.

4. Turn the paper right side up, then gather the folds together as shown. The concertina will change direction when it meets the diagonal fold, but as the folds were pre-creased in both directions this should happen fairly easily.

## Instructions

5. Repeat Steps 1-4 with the second A4 sheet, then join the two sheets together along a short edge, using washi tape to help the concertina folds link together smoothly.

6. Use the hole punch to add holes 1cm (⅜") down from the top long edge of the lantern, creating one hole per section of concertina.

7. Bring the two short edges of the lantern together, creating a circle. Join together with washi tape, as per Step 5, then thread the ribbon through the punched holes. Pull the ends together carefully, gathering the concertina at the top, then knot to secure.

8. To finish, place an LED tealight under the lantern.

# REINDEER GARLAND

### Materials

- Brother ScanNCut (optional)
- Adhesive mat
- Paper
- Christmas Garland templates
- Twine
- Adhesive gems
- Small pompoms
- Jingle bells
- Adhesives

## Instructions

1.

First, download the SVG or PDF files to make your own Christmas Garland.

2.

Use the templates to cut out all the shapes from coloured card. Using the traditional method simply download the PDF and use to trace the shapes on to card.

3.

Using a clear drying glue, attach the antlers, hooves and an eye to each of the nine deer. Attach noses to eight of the deer

4.

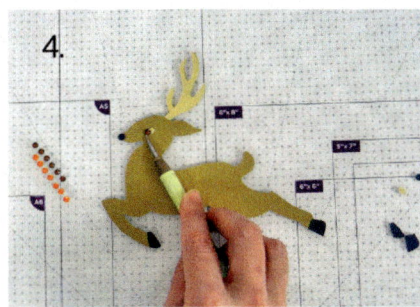

Optional, add a pale brown or orange adhesive gem to each of the deer's eyes.

5.

Line up and glue yellow sleigh trim onto the sleigh.

6.

Line up and glue Santa's beard onto his face and then onto the main sleigh piece. Attach hat trim, hat bobble and glove to hand.

Add some pale blue adhesive gems as eyes (or you can use the provided cutting shapes to cut eyes from blue card if preferred)

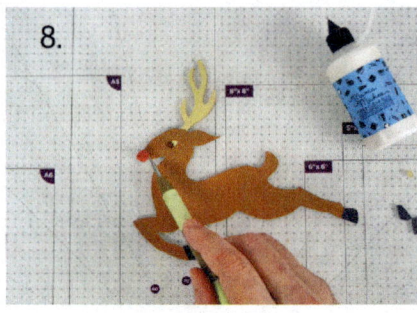

Glue a small red pompom onto one of the deer (this one will be Rudolph!) and a white pompom to Santas hat, if desired.

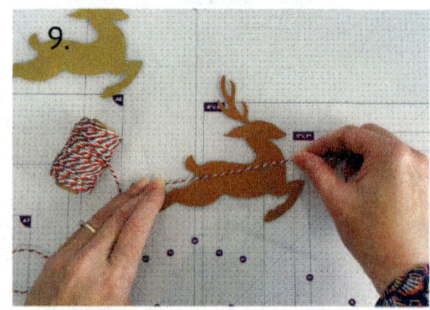

Alternatively, place a small piece of tape over the twine to secure your sleigh and reindeer.

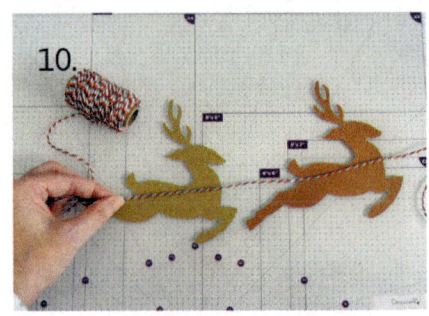

Take another deer and turn over, so still working on the reverse and repeat, adding a line of tape as before, pressing firmly to secure.

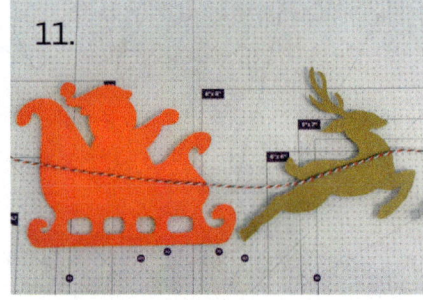

Attach the sleigh in the same way, adding a line of red liner tape and pressing down firmly to secure. Ensure you leave an overhang of twine before cutting it, to provide enough for hanging loops.

To add extra detail and a fun element, thread two small white jingle bells onto some twine and attach them to the sleigh. Add another bell threaded onto twine around Rudolph's neck if desired.

# CONCLUSION

Welcome to "Papercrafting Christmas Ideas: Magical Christmas Crafts for All Ages" This book welcomes you to the magical realm of papercrafting, where festive passion and creativity collide. There has never been a better moment to embrace the love of making and produce stunning and unforgettable creations that infuse your house with warmth and cheer than during the enchantment of Christmas.

More than just a pastime, crafting over the holidays is a great way to connect with loved ones and show your creativity. Every paper creation you make has the potential to develop into a treasured custom that is carried down through the generations. Whether you're creating tree-hanging ornaments, creating sentimental Christmas cards, or creatively wrapping presents, every little thing counts.

This book contains comprehensive directions, practical advice, and motivational ideas to help you make beautiful Christmas crafts. Every chapter covers a different facet of papercrafting, ranging from eco-friendly alternatives and gift wrapping to cards and decorations. Your creativity will be able to blossom as you master vital techniques, find new materials, and experiment with other styles.

Welcome to the wonderful world of Christmas papercrafting! Let's get started on this magical adventure!

Printed in Dunstable, United Kingdom